UNLEASHED

Frances R. Sheridan

UNLEASHED

The Dog Runs of New York City

PRESTEL

MUNICH · BERLIN · LONDON · NEW YORK

MANHATTAN   19

Man and dog have been living together for at least fifteen thousand years. For much of the time they have also made their living together. Wherever people went to work, dogs were usually at their sides. Hunting, herding, and guarding were among the many chores that filled a dog's day. These activities provided dogs with both physical and mental exercise, and after a long hard day, human and canine could look forward to a well-deserved night's rest. The world of work has changed dramatically for people and their dogs over the past several decades. Dog ownership has soared while the number of available canine careers has diminished. Most people now find that their work requires the help of a mouse, not a dog. While retirement is a well-deserved dream that many of us envision after a long life of work, no one wants to be retired in their prime. But, that is just the fate that has befallen most dogs. No longer needed to pursue game, herd sheep, or guard flocks, dogs are too often left to a home life that has them hunting sunbeams, herding furniture, and waiting for mom and dad to come home. While some dogs adapt to this new line of work, others deteriorate both physically and psychologically. This problem has been most serious for dogs living in urban environments. The lack of backyards and other open spaces has made it difficult for people to provide the exercise that helps to keep a dog's body and mind stimulated and sound. A new type of urban cultural center has evolved to fulfill this need for dogs and their people—the dog run.

Dotted throughout the city in various parks and public spaces, dog runs have become the place where dogs can be dogs. Here, with no furniture or carpets, they can run, chase, and play with wild abandon. They engage in mock-serious battles that are punctuated by the doggie equivalent of a grin and a giggle—the play bow, which signals "gotcha, I was just fooling around"—which usually presages another roundabout chase ending in a panting, tongue-flapping heap at your feet. A few moments rest and they are off again to cavort with another of their canine cohorts. Perhaps they will cast a sideways glance and catch your eye as they engage in that most frequently inhibited canine pleasure—peeing wherever they want. Finally, when they come back to you with that glow of being "good tired" they do not so much submit to the leash as they solicit it for a relaxing walk home and a comfy nap.

As much fun as all this is for the dogs and people, it is a valuable antidote to the lack of purpose many dogs may have. It gives them a chance to express their full "dogginess." While they are adept at living within the world of people, playing with other dogs gives them a chance to communicate in fluent canine. The games they play with other dogs and their people provide today's pooches with the psychological stimulation they need to remain alert and retain their mental health. Continuing behavioral research on canine behavior will likely show that, similar to data available for people, an active and diverse mental life helps to protect against a decline in cognitive function as dogs age. At the same time, these shared activities strengthen and enrich the bond between dogs and their people. A bond that will enhance the good times, and help them through the challenges that may come along.

Dogs and humans have a great part of their recent evolution invested in one another. Their journey has crisscrossed the globe from field to pasture and from tropical to urban jungle. Happily that journey now includes a stroll down to the local dog run for some time in the sun.

ATTENTION OFF-LEASH DOG AREA

WELCOME
By entering this dog run, you agree to follow our rules.
Please read them.
(Rules are posted next to this gate and inside the run.)

Dog Run
←

THIS RUN IS FOR SMALL DOG ONLY
DOGS OVER 25 LBS. ARE NOT PERMITTED
IF YOUR DOG WEIGHS MORE THAN 25... PLEASE USE THE A... BIG DOG RUN

MAINTENANCE OF THIS SITE AND ITS PERIMETER IS THE RESPONSIBILITY OF THOSE WHO USE IT
PLEASE CLEAN UP AFTER YOUR DOG AND KEEP THE PARK CLEAN
City of New York Parks and Recreation
Rudolph W. Giuliani, Mayor
Henry J. Stern, Commissioner

NO 1ST PEES
(till the grafs). Pleas?.

DOG RUN
PLEASE CLEAN UP AFTER YOUR DOG

If You're Not Responsible Enough To Clean Up After Your Dog, You Don't Deserve To Own One
www.nyc.gov/parks

STOP & READ
FOR THE SAFTY OF OUR DOGS, PLEASE OPEN ONE GATE AT A TIME.
KEEP OUR DOG RUN CLEAN. WATCH & CLEAN UP AFTER YOUR DOG !

OFF LEASH DOG AREA
↑

NEW
SMALL DOG AREA
Entrance Just Round The Bend
⇢⇢⇢⇢⇢⇢⇢⇢⇢⇢

Love Your Pet, Love Your Park
License, leash, and clean up after your d... It's the law.
www.nyc.gov/parks

DOG RUN AREA
→

ST. GEORGE CANINE ASSN.
AT ST. PETER'S CHURCH
A MEMBER MAINTAINED
DOG RUN
IF INTERESTED... JOIN US SUNDAYS 9AM

TRIBECA DOG OWNERS
DOG RUN

THIS SPACE designated for the exercise of dogs and their owners only

↑
TO DOG RUN

BATTERY PARK CITY
PARKS
CORPORATION

PLEAS PICK UP AFTER YOUR PET

New York City is full of surprises. One morning on Manhattan's busy Upper East Side, I noticed what resembled a baby black bear heading in my direction. Soon at my feet wriggled a puppy Rottweiler. She had left her mother's side for the first time and scampered down the sidewalk to me. With a poke of her nose I was designated her rightful owner. I called her Indy.

That encounter sparked a life-long adventure. Indy led us into the New York dog world. We joined the pack that frequents the city's dog runs and discovered how active urban canine communities meet, greet, romp, roll, run, exercise, and socialize on a daily basis.

Together, we sought out unleashed canine activity all over the city. Indy inspected and tested New York City's dog runs, using her own four-paw rating system of canine criteria, while I observed the expressions of the unleashed dog's freedom in photographs. These unwrangled images will introduce you to some of New York's magnificent everyday dogs.

You are invited to take a tour of New York City's unique dog runs with Indy, an insider.

Meet the dogs online at *www.unleashedthebook.com*

DEFINING DOG RUNS

A "dog run" is a designated area where people can let their dogs play unleashed. Some runs are private and require membership. Most are public and can be found in our parks. When an entire park is fenced or a leash-free zone, it is called a "dog park." Dog owners form or join groups that manage dog runs in conjunction with city officials. Run users contribute funds and volunteer help to maintain their dog runs. Suggested donations typically range from $10 to $40 per year, but dog runs located outside public parks may have higher membership fees to meet higher costs. Many dog owner groups are not-for-profit, making donations tax-deductible.

The American Kennel Club makes the following points about the benefits provided by a run to dogs, their owners, and the community as a whole.

MORE THAN JUST "ROOM TO ROAM," THE CREATION OF A DOG RUN:

* **ALLOWS DOGS TO EXERCISE AND SOCIALIZE SAFELY** Puppies and adult dogs need room to run, and enclosed play areas permit them to do so while preventing them from endangering themselves and others. In addition, dogs who are accustomed to playing with animals and people other than their owners are more likely to be well socialized and react well toward strangers.

* **PROMOTES RESPONSIBLE DOG OWNERSHIP** Dog runs prevent off-leash animals from infringing on the rights of other community residents and park users such as joggers, small children, and those who may be fearful of dogs.

* **PROVIDES AN OUTLET FOR DOG OWNERS TO SOCIALIZE** Dog runs are a great place for owners to meet other people with common interests. The love people share for their dogs reaches beyond economic and social barriers and helps to foster a sense of community.

* **MAKES FOR A BETTER COMMUNITY BY PROMOTING PUBLIC HEALTH AND SAFETY** Well-exercised dogs are better neighbors who are less likely to create a nuisance, bark excessively, and destroy property. Their presence in the park, along with their owners, also helps to deter crime.

The Carl Schurz Dog Run Committee highlights another beneficial use of dog runs. Carl's run is lent to local shelter dogs and their handlers during designated hours each week. This time of socializing and sanctuary helps alleviate fear and boredom, increasing the orphans' adoptability. Plus, potential adopters gain the opportunity to see the dogs at play and better evaluate their temperaments.

MAINTAINING GOOD HEALTH

Having a dog in the city is complicated and necessitates committing to walk your pet 3 or 4 times a day unless you have a dog-walker or the assistance of multiple family members. Except in the case of inclement weather, this is beneficial for both the owners and their dogs.

There are many ways in which exercise may benefit your dog. Playing tag in the dog run and toppling over other dogs improves its muscle tone, endurance, and the other cardiac related aspects of its health. A nice workout for one's pet also stimulates normalcy of the gastrointestinal tract. Allowing your dog to play in the dog run provides a social benefit for you both, the only exception being when your dog is a bully. It is becoming commonplace in dog runs to have two separate sections, one of which is designated for small dogs in order to help avoid altercations. If you own an aggressive dog, you may want to choose jogging with your dog as an alternative exercise to using a dog run.

There are potential medical drawbacks to using a dog run, although most are minor and easily preventable. It is possible to contract infectious diseases such as kennel cough, upper respiratory infections including distemper virus, or gastrointestinal viruses, more specifically corona virus or parvovirus. Parvovirus is a life-threatening illness, however, you can prevent against it by making certain your dog is fully vaccinated prior to playing at the dog runs. Puppies need to complete their entire vaccination series before dog run exposure. It is important to remember that a pet does not receive immediate immunity at the time of the last vaccination. There is a two-week lag phase before it is safe to expose your pup to the dog run or the streets of New York City! Other diseases that your pet must be vaccinated against are rabies, distemper/parvo (DA2P-PV) and possibly bordetella (Kennel Cough). Rabies vaccine is mandatory by law. If your unvaccinated dog bites another dog, it will need to be quarantined for ten days to observe for any symptoms of rabies. This is mandated by the Department of Health.

Dermatologic problems could also arise from exposure to fleas and ticks. There are, however, very effective topical preventatives to help avoid these annoyances. Ringworm, a fungal disease that can cause patchy areas of hair loss, can be contracted from spores, which are present in the environment from infected pets. The good news is that usually only immuno-suppressed dogs will be affected by this organism. If your pet is known to have an incompetent immune system, it should not frequent dog runs.

Dogs may also be exposed to gastrointestinal parasites such as roundworms, hookworms, whipworms, coccidia, and giardia by coming into contact with other dogs' feces. It only requires a microscopic piece of stool to get on your pet's paw and then be licked off to contract these parasites. Most parasites will not be contracted if your pet is taking a monthly heartworm preventative year-round. Not all heartworm preventatives provide the same gastrointestinal parasite control, so be sure to discuss with your vet the need to protect your pet from parasites at the dog run.

Although there may be several potential medical risks in having your pet play at a dog run, most can be prevented with vaccination and parasite prevention. Except in the case of a severe dog bite wound or parvo infection, most ailments can be easily treated by your veterinarian. The benefits of exercise and the ability to prolong the life of your pet far outnumber the risks encountered at the dog run given that your pet is healthy and has a competent immune system.

New York dogs are required to wear a city license (obtained from the Health Department, www.nyc.gov/health) along with their rabies and identification tags. In addition to what dogs wear, there are rules regarding the places they visit. Check the specific rules of the dog run you will be attending and observe them. Here are some basic rules that help to make dog runs safe and pleasant places to visit.

* **DOGS MUST BE HEALTHY** Dogs must be current on their rabies shots, vaccinations, and be free of parasites.

* **NO PUPPIES LESS THAN 4 MONTHS OLD** Even if they have had their shots, they are still susceptible to disease.

* **FIRST TIME RUN USERS SHOULD VISIT DURING OFF-PEAK HOURS** Meeting the curiosity and welcome of a lot of canines during peak hours can be stressful on initial visits.

* **UNLEASH YOUR DOG AS SOON AS YOU ARRIVE** Leashed dogs may feel threatened and act in an aggressive manner when unleashed dogs greet them.

* **REMOVE CHOKE / PINCH COLLARS AT GATE** Use buckle or snap collars inside the run. Choke / Pinch collars can hook onto objects or other dogs, causing choking and/or violent fighting.

* **SUPERVISE YOUR DOG** Ensure proper socialization by watching your dog at all times to see with whom he's playing and how they are getting along. Prevent problems by addressing the beginnings of behavior that will need your interference and restructure.

* **ALWAYS CLEAN UP AFTER YOUR DOG** Encourage others by setting a good example through your own model behavior.

* **DO NOT BRING FOOD FOR PEOPLE OR DOGS INTO THE RUN** The presence of food can start a dogfight.

* **REFRAIN YOUR DOG FROM SUSTAINED BARKING** It can bother neighbors, especially during early mornings and late evenings.

* **NO MORE THAN THREE DOGS PER PERSON IN THE RUN** More than three becomes too difficult to monitor properly and pick up after.

* **IMMEDIATELY BREAK UP FIGHTS** Do not panic. Owners should grasp their dogs' hind legs and pull the canines away from each other.

* **DO NOT BRING YOUNG CHILDREN INTO THE RUN** Prevent injuries by not placing your children in an environment with rough playing dogs. If you are in a run that allows children you must assume all responsibility in case of injury.

* **NO BITCHES IN HEAT ALLOWED IN RUN** Plus, un-neutered males must be extra carefully supervised and removed upon signs of making other dogs uncomfortable by aggressive or amorous displays.

LEGENDS

 dog run locator

 shade: umbrellas, awnings, trees, etc.

 poop pick-ups: baggies, shovels, rakes, etc.

 benches

 water source

 canine pool

 seperate area for little dogs

 garbage cans

 double gated entry

 dog wash hose

 agility equipment

 lights

 membership required

 tables

INDY'S PAW RATING SYSTEM

bare bones run

good run

great run

a place where it is a pleasure
to put four paws down

NEW YORK CITY RUN SIZES

SMALL RUN
less than 5,000 square feet

MEDIUM RUN
5,000 to 14,000 square feet

LARGE RUN
more than 14,000 square feet

THE
BRONX

MANHATTAN

QUEENS

BROOKLYN

STATEN
ISLAND

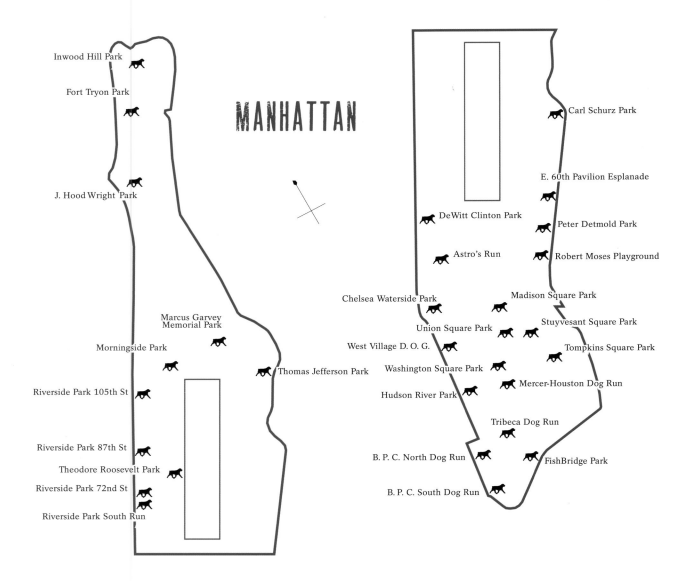

MANHATTAN

Inwood Hill Park

Fort Tryon Park

J. Hood Wright Park

Carl Schurz Park

E. 60th Pavilion Esplanade

DeWitt Clinton Park

Peter Detmold Park

Astro's Run

Robert Moses Playground

Marcus Garvey
Memorial Park

Chelsea Waterside Park

Madison Square Park

Morningside Park

Union Square Park

Stuyvesant Square Park

West Village D. O. G.

Tompkins Square Park

Thomas Jefferson Park

Washington Square Park

Riverside Park 105th St

Hudson River Park

Mercer-Houston Dog Run

Tribeca Dog Run

Riverside Park 87th St

Theodore Roosevelt Park

B. P. C. North Dog Run

FishBridge Park

Riverside Park 72nd St

Riverside Park South Run

B. P. C. South Dog Run

Manhattan played host to Indy's first dog run experiences. Her large puppy personality and boundless energy could not be contained in our small New York apartment. A place to let loose was a necessity. We became assiduous explorers of New York's green oases, and quickly found inviting spaces where Indy could run. A sense of community, fostered through an ongoing dialogue with other dog lovers, welcomed us at local dog runs. Indy's life as a puppy was full of happy, unleashed activities that continued into her dreams, paws running in the air while fast asleep.

Tompkins Square Park is home to our first dog run as well as New York City's aptly-named First Run. A tree sculpture in the run's center stands adorned with dog tags, a memorial to good friends and times. There Indy discovered a fascination with rubber balls, not her own, mind you, but those she could grab and run away with, happily chased by the rightful owner and his cohort. Indy went on to test the city's proliferating and popular runs, accumulating in the process an impressive collection of dog-toy trophies, generously donated by less stubborn visitors.

Dog runs in Manhattan have evolved from their bare-boned "dirt and fence" beginnings in the early '90s, to posh playgrounds in some parks. Today's runs often have amenities that make them pleasing to visit for both dogs and people. For instance, the latest run, K-9 Sirius (under construction at the time of writing), in Battery Park City's Monsignor Kowsky Plaza, is designed around the recent discovery that dogs can see in color.

Such elaborate treatment extends to other realms of dog life as well. In bustling Manhattan, doggie social calendars can quickly fill with engagements. In addition to play dates at the local dog run, Manhattan dogs may go on regular outings with a dog walker or to doggie daycare. Some visit groomers, spas, or dog camps while others participate in playgroups, obedience classes, and agility trials.

There are a number of dog-friendly establishments to visit in Manhattan, although some are restricted to portable pups. The Cathedral of St. John the Divine, among others, invites dogs to attend church each year for the Blessing of the Animals, held in October. The religious service celebrates the Feast Day of St. Francis, the Patron Saint of Animals.

Throughout the year, breed fanciers host gatherings of their dogs of a kind and holidays are celebrated with festive fundraisers to support dog runs and shelters. Many of the special events hosted by animal lovers to promote adoption and responsible pet ownership draw celebrity support and first-chop entertainment. To find out more about adoption days, shelter fundraisers, and other animal events happening throughout New York City, visit the Mayor's Alliance for NYC's Animals at www.animalalliancenyc.org.

INWOOD HILL DOG RUN

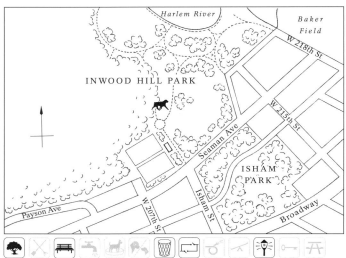

This park offers interesting trails to explore and its run provides ample space for a game of retrieval with a high flung ball.

PARK Inwood Hill Park

LOCATION Seaman Avenue and Isham Street

HOURS Dawn to Dusk

SIZE Medium

GROUND Pea Gravel

To get involved in caring for this dog run contact:

The Partnerships for Parks Outreach Coordinator for this Park

ADDRESS c/o Partnerships for Parks,

830 Fifth Avenue—The Arsenal,

New York, NY 10021

TEL (212) 408 0230

WEBSITE www.partnershipsforparks.org

SIR WILLIAM'S DOG RUN

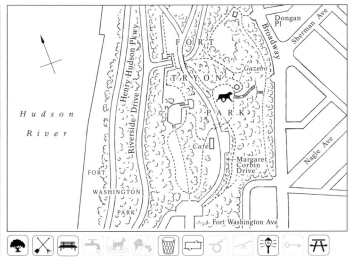

Canine exuberance abounds in this lovely, well-maintained dog run.

PARK Fort Tryon Park

LOCATION Downstairs at parking lot across from Café at

1 Margaret Corbin Drive

HOURS 6 A.M. to 1 A.M.

SIZE Large

GROUND Wood Chips

DOG OWNERS GROUP FTDOG (Fort Tryon Dog Owners Group)

DONATIONS P.O. Box 750, New York, NY 10040

CONTACT Jennifer Bristol

E-MAIL jennftdog@aol.com

WEBSITE www.ftdog.org

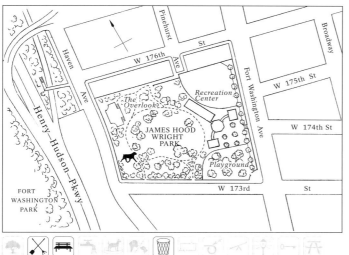

PARK J. Hood Wright Park

LOCATION West 173rd Street and Haven Avenue

HOURS Dawn to Dusk

SIZE Small

GROUND Pea Gravel

To get involved in caring for this dog run contact:

The Partnerships for Parks Outreach Coordinator for this Park

ADDRESS c/o Partnerships for Parks,

830 Fifth Avenue—The Arsenal,

New York, NY 10021

TEL (212) 408 0230

WEBSITE www.partnershipsforparks.org

Members of the neighborhood here pitch in to help keep the run clean. A community generosity appreciated by all.

MORNINGSIDE PARK DOG RUN

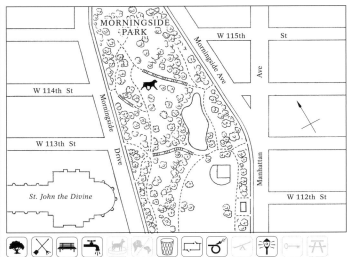

This run has united a diverse community and become a flourishing gathering spot. It is a fine example of how efforts can be rewarding beyond expectations.

PARK Morningside Park

LOCATION West 114th Street and Morningside Drive

HOURS 6 A.M. to 10 P.M.

SIZE Large

GROUND Wood Chips

DOG OWNERS GROUP Morningside BARC (Build a Run Coalition)

DONATIONS P.O. Box 1765, Morningside Station, New York, NY 10026

CONTACTS Dottie Janotka, Barbara Leese, Gail Karp, Joyce Rushing Reid (co-chairs of the group)

E-MAIL morningsideBARC_Exec@yahoogroups.com

BULLETINS morningsidebarc@yahoogroups.com

WEBSITE www.morningsidebarc.org

MARCUS' DOG RUN

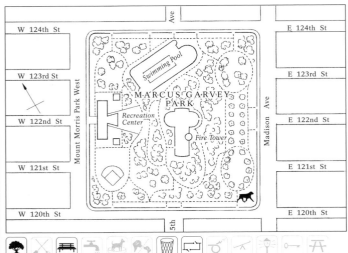

The location and size of this run will enable it to rank with the best dog runs in the city when it receives some sprucing up.

PARK Marcus Garvey Memorial Park

LOCATION Madison Avenue and East 120th Street

HOURS Dawn to Dusk

SIZE Medium

GROUND Wood Chips

To get involved in caring for this dog run contact:

The Partnerships for Parks Outreach Coordinator for this Park

ADDRESS c/o Partnerships for Parks,

830 Fifth Avenue—The Arsenal,

New York, NY 10021

TEL (212) 408 0230

WEBSITE www.partnershipsforparks.org

TOM'S DOG RUN

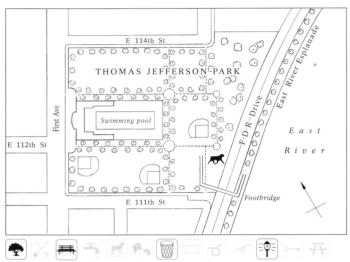

The FDR Drive roars by this triangular-shaped run. Nevertheless, the opportunity to socialize remains paramount.

PARK Thomas Jefferson Park

LOCATION East 112th Street and First Avenue

HOURS Dawn to Dusk

SIZE Small

GROUND Wood Chips

To get involved in caring for this dog run contact:

The Partnerships for Parks Outreach Coordinator for this Park

ADDRESS c/o Partnerships for Parks,

830 Fifth Avenue—The Arsenal,

New York, NY 10021

TEL (212) 408 0230

WEBSITE www.partnershipsforparks.org

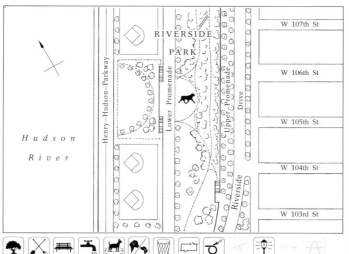

PARK Riverside Park

LOCATION Riverside Drive and 105th Street

HOURS 6 A.M. to 1 A.M.

SIZE Medium

GROUND Crushed Gravel

OWNERS GROUP Riverside Park Dog Owners Group

ADDRESS c/o Riverside Park Fund,

475 Riverside Drive, Suite 455,

New York, NY 10115

CONTACT John Herrold

TEL via the Riverside Park Fund, (212) 870 3070

A wide array of dog breeds play in this beautifully appointed run. It is a model for dog runs, exhibiting a blend of elegance and function.

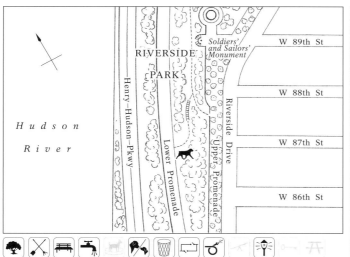

PARK Riverside Park

LOCATION Riverside Drive and 87th Street

HOURS 6 A.M. to 1 A.M.

SIZE Medium

GROUND Crushed Bluestone

DOG OWNER GROUP 87th Street Dog Run Group

DONATIONS c/o Riverside Park Fund, 475 Riverside Drive, Suite 455, New York, NY 10115

CONTACT Brett Kopelan

TEL via the Riverside Park Fund, (212) 870 3070

BULLETINS dogrun87@yahoogroups.com

WEBSITE www.dogrun87.org

This well-kept run has an open area and a grouping of trees that dogs like to run around, sniff, and play under.

72ND STREET DOG RUN

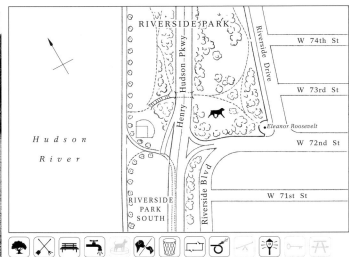

The dedicated dog owners here help to keep this run clean and beautiful. Renovations are underway to update it with improvements for the benefit of area dogs and the neighborhood.

PARK Riverside Park

LOCATION Riverside Drive and West 72nd Street

HOURS 7 A.M. to 10 P.M.

SIZE Large

GROUND Straw

DOG OWNER GROUP Friends and Lovers Of Riverside Area Life (FLORAL)

DONATIONS c/o Riverside Park Fund, 475 Riverside Drive, Suite 455, New York, NY 10115

CONTACT Jeffrey Zahn

TEL via the Riverside Park Fund, (212) 870 3070

E-MAIL info@rspfloral.org

WEBSITE www.rspfloral.org

RIVERSIDE SOUTH DOG RUN

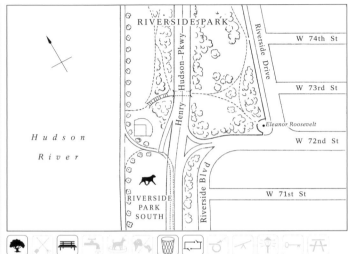

An overhead highway lends a bold architectural element to this basic run, conveniently located in a rapidly developing neighborhood.

PARK Riverside Park

LOCATION West 72nd Street, under the West Side Highway

HOURS 7 A.M. to 11 P.M.

SIZE Small

GROUND Wood Chips

To get involved in caring for this dog run contact:

Park Manager Jibrail Nor

ADDRESS c/o Riverside Park Fund,

475 Riverside Drive, Suite 455,

New York, NY 10115

TEL (212) 408 0265, or via the Riverside Park Fund (212) 870 3070

E-MAIL jibrail.nor@parks.nyc.gov

TEDDY'S DOG RUN

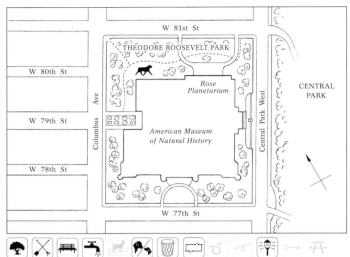

The well-collared set plays in this run, which is nestled near the Rose Center for Earth and Space's Hayden Planetarium. It is nicely equipped to make visits "out of this world" for dogs and people.

PARK Theodore Roosevelt Park

LOCATION West 81st Street and Columbus Avenue

HOURS 7 A.M. to 10 P.M.

SIZE Medium

GROUND Crushed Granite

DOG OWNER GROUP The Friends of Museum Park Dog Run

DONATIONS P.O. Box 412, Planetarium Station, New York, NY 10024

CONTACT Richard Gordon

V-MAIL (212) 946 4542

E-MAIL rmg4dogs@aol.com

CARL'S DOG RUN

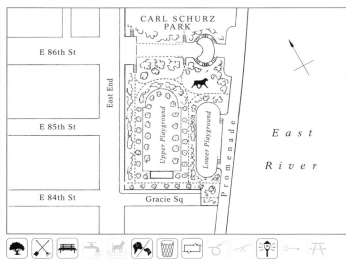

*Separate runs for large and small dogs
in a serene setting are kept clean and
welcoming to the delight of dogs on their
outings.*

PARK Carl Schurz Park

LOCATION East 86th Street and East End

HOURS Dawn to Dusk

SIZE Medium

GROUND Pea Gravel, Decking

DOG OWNER GROUP The Dog Run Committee

ADDRESS c/o Carl Schurz Park Association, P. O. Box 116,
217 East 85th Street, New York, NY 10028

CONTACT Samantha Schmidt

TEL (212) 737 0065

E-MAIL sjs@nyc.rr.com

WEBSITE www.carlschurzparknyc.org

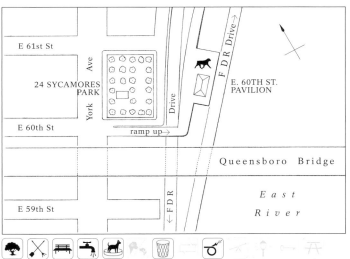

PARK E. 60th Street Pavilion Esplanade

LOCATION East 60th Street, above the FDR Drive

HOURS Dawn to Dusk

SIZE Small

GROUND Cement

To get involved in caring for this dog run contact:

The Partnerships for Parks Outreach Coordinator for this Park

ADDRESS c/o Partnerships for Parks,

830 Fifth Avenue—The Arsenal,

New York, NY 10021

TEL (212) 408 0216

WEBSITE www.partnershipsforparks.org

A spectacular view of the 59th Street Bridge can be enjoyed from this agreeable run, which is visited by an abundance of local dogs and their owners.

PDP-ARF DOG RUN

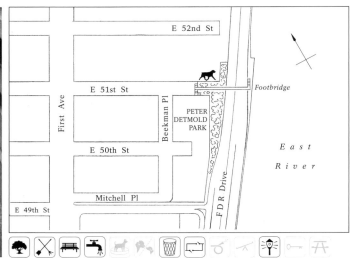

Some dogs here have formed lifelong friendships, showing up daily for standing appointments. This is a nicely maintained dog run, situated against the clamor of the FDR Drive.

PARK Peter Detmold Park

LOCATION East 51st Street and Beekman Place

HOURS Dawn to Dusk

SIZE Medium

GROUND Cement

USER GROUP PDP-ARF, Inc. (Peter Detmold Park—Animals Run Free)

DONATIONS c/o Mara, 120 East 56th Street, New York, NY 10022

CONTACT Geri Van Rees

TEL (212) 758 8255

E-MAIL gvr@prodigy.net

ROBERT'S DOG RUN

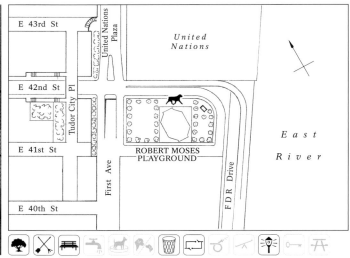

This clean, basic run provides an important opportunity for socialization and fun for the friendly dog community in this area.

PARK Robert Moses Playground

LOCATION East 42nd Street and 1st Avenue

HOURS Dawn to Dusk

SIZE Small

GROUND Concrete

To get involved in caring for this dog run contact:

The Partnerships for Parks Outreach Coordinator for this Park

ADDRESS c/o Partnerships for Parks,

830 Fifth Avenue—The Arsenal,

New York, NY 10021

TEL (212) 408 0216

WEBSITE www.partnershipsforparks.org

DEWITT'S DOG RUN

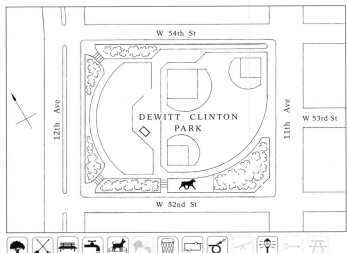

Dog owners have created a safe, well-furnished dog run that serves as a real oasis for dogs and their owners in this park.

PARK DeWitt Clinton Park

LOCATION West 52nd Street and 11th Avenue

HOURS 7 A.M. to 10 P.M.

SIZE Medium

GROUND Cement

DOG OWNER GROUP Friends of Dewitt Clinton Dog Run

BULLETINS dewittdog@yahoogroups.com

WEBSITE www.dogrun.org

ASTRO'S DOG RUN

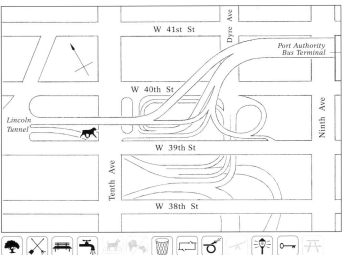

A bright spot of refuge in a gray tangle of streets and traffic, this run is an excellent use of a small space. Dogs enjoy visiting and take full advantage of their time here.

PLACE Astro's Community Garden and Dog Run

LOCATION West 39th Street and 10th Avenue

HOURS Dawn to Dusk

RUN SIZE Small

GROUND Argulite, Red Clay

DOG OWNER GROUP Hell's Kitchen Neighborhood Association

ADDRESS c/o Community Board 4,
330 West 42nd Street, New York, NY 10036

CONTACT Francis Daily

TEL via community board 4 (212) 736 4536

E-MAIL hkdogrun39@aol.com

WEBSITE www.astrosdogrun.com

MEMBERSHIP $15 Annual Dues

🐾🐾🐾🐾

This is the first run to be designed into a park's primary plans. This run enlivens an otherwise unpleasant triangle area between busy streets. Dogs enjoy playing in the fun landscape of this run.

PARK Chelsea Waterside Park
LOCATION West 23rd Street and 11th Avenue
HOURS 7 A.M. to 1 A.M.
SIZE Small
GROUND Cement
DOG OWNER GROUP West Chelsea Dog Owners Group
DONATIONS 200 West 20th Street, Apt. 208, New York, NY 10011
CONTACT Doris Corrigan
TEL (212) 924 5433
E-MAIL mdcorrigan@aol.com
WEBSITE www.bitsworld.com/dogrun

JEMMY'S DOG RUN

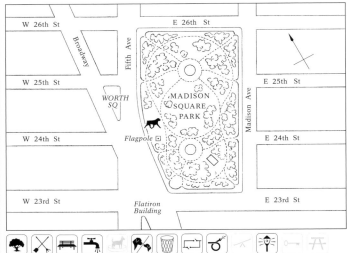

In a beautifully renovated park, this popular run is kept clean, well furnished, and welcoming to many different local breeds and a variety of canine personalities.

PARK Madison Square Park

LOCATION 24th Street and Fifth Avenue

HOURS 6 A.M. to 12 P.M.

SIZE Small

GROUND Pea Gravel

USER GROUP Friends of Jemmy's Dog Run

DONATIONS P.O. Box 1119, Madison Square Station, New York, NY 10159

CONTACT Ira Herman

TEL (212) 408 5469

E-MAIL iherman@chadbourne.com

STUYVESANT DOG RUN

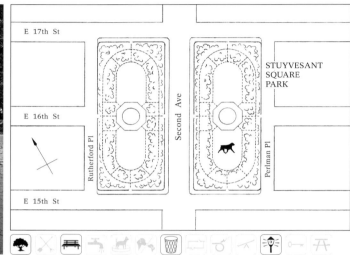

This is one of the most unique runs in the city due to its part-time schedule. Only during specific morning and evening hours a section of the park is fenced off for unleashed dog play. The responsible dog owners here prove that this is an effective way to share public park space.

PARK Stuyvesant Square Park

LOCATION East 15th Street and 2nd Avenue

HOURS Part-time: 7–9 A.M. Mon.–Fri., 7–11 A.M. Sat.–Sun., 9–11 P.M. All Evenings

SIZE Small

GROUND Cobblestone

DOG OWNER GROUP SPDOG (Stuyvesant Park Dog Owners Group)

DONATIONS c/o SPDOG Treasurer, P.O. Box 1767, Madison Square Station, New York, NY 10159

CONTACTS J. Ludwig, A. Kner

TEL (212) 777 2556

E-MAIL jludwig@nyc.rr.com

BULLETINS http://groups.msn.com/spdog

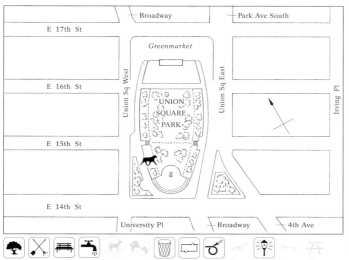

PARK Union Square Park

LOCATION West 15th Street and Union Square West

HOURS 6 A.M. to 12 P.M.

SIZE Small

GROUND Brownstone Screenings

DOG OWNER GROUP Friends of Union Square Dog Run Association

CONTACTS Nicole Barth and David Kim

E-MAIL unionsquaredogrun@hotmail.com

WEBSITE www.uniondog.org

Passersby line the fence to watch the playful pups in action at this run in the heart of busy Union Square. The dog owners group here has made significant improvements in the run, making it a favorite destination for many dogs and their owners.

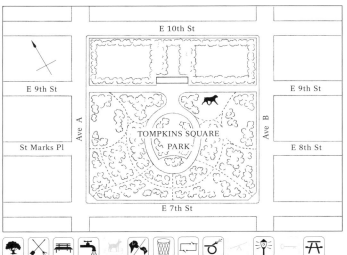

PARK Tompkins Square Park

LOCATION East 9th Street and Avenue B

HOURS 6 A.M. to 12 P.M.

SIZE Large

GROUND Wood Chips

DOG OWNER GROUP Friends of First Run

DONATIONS 503 East 6th Street, Apt. 3R, New York, NY 10009

CONTACT Garrett Rosso

TEL (212) 522 3298, (212) 522 2769

E-MAIL firstrun-nyc-owner@yahoogroups.com

WEBSITE www.dogster.org

Devoted dog owners keep this spacious run clean and loaded with doggie details. The Small Dog Area lets the little ones enjoy play with equal-sized friends.

WASHINGTON SQUARE DOG RUN

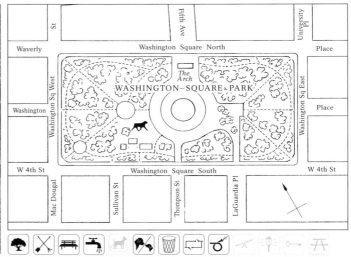

The area's numerous resident dogs keep this run packed with pups during peak hours. The separate Robin Kovary Run for Small Dogs offers a safe haven for the play of the little ones.

PARK Washington Square Park

LOCATION Thompson Street and Washington Square South

HOURS 6 A.M. to 12 P.M.

SIZE Small

GROUND Pearl Gravel Mix

DOG OWNER GROUP Washington Square Dog Run Association

DONATIONS 7 East 8th Street, Suite 341, New York, NY 10003

CONTACT Pat McKee

TEL (212) 560 4345

WEBSITE www.washsqdogrun.org

LITTLE RUN Robin Kovary Run for Small Dogs

CONTACT Louise Symonds

E-MAIL smalldogrun@nyc.rr.com

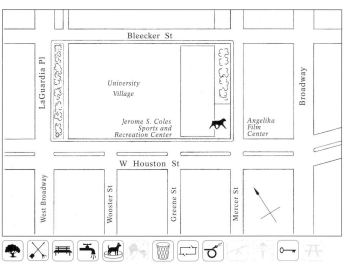

LOCATION Mercer and West Houston Streets

HOURS Dawn to Dusk

SIZE Small

GROUND Cement

DOG OWNER GROUP Mercer-Houston Dog Run Association, Inc.

MEMBERSHIP APPLICATIONS 532 LaGuardia Place, #178,
New York, NY 10012

E-MAIL info@mhdra.org

WEBSITE www.mhdra.org

MEMBERSHIP $50 Annual Dues

Canine members of this well-maintained run enjoy added amenities such as a continuous supply of balls for sharing and a pool big enough for two.

WEST VILLAGE DOG RUN

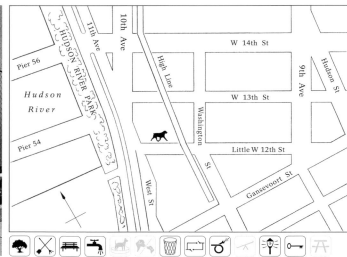

This urban run is kept clean and stocked with amenities. For local dogs, it serves as a city-style "backyard" hangout. The membership waiting list testifies to the importance New Yorkers place on the well-being of their canines.

LOCATION Little West 12th Street and 10th Avenue

HOURS Dawn to Dusk

SIZE Small

GROUND Asphalt Paving

DOG OWNER GROUP West Village D.O.G. (Dog Owners Group), Inc.

DONATIONS 41 Bethune Street, New York, NY 10014

CONTACT Tracey Sides

TEL (212) 807 0093

E-MAIL wvdog1@aol.com

WEBSITE www.wvdog.org

MEMBERSHIP $40 Annual Dues

PIER 40 RIVER RUN

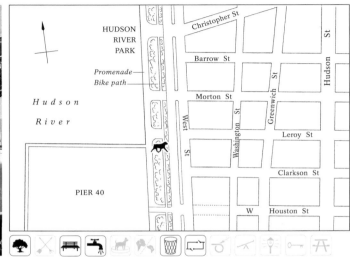

The dog-owner community here is trying to make improvements to this run so that it becomes a pleasant, and safe play zone for the area's numerous dogs.

PARK Hudson River Park

LOCATION West and Leroy Streets

HOURS Dawn to Dusk

SIZE Small

GROUND Coated Cement

DOG OWNER GROUP DOAC (Dog Owners Action Committee)

CONTACT Lynn Pacifico

E-MAIL lynnpax@earthlink.net

BULLETINS www.pulitzer.com/dogrunwho.html

TRIBECA DOG RUN

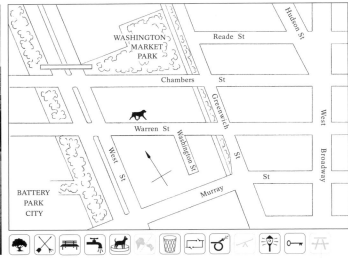

Assorted canine characters engage in leash-less antics to amuse themselves at this well-provisioned and kept run.

LOCATION Warren and West Streets

HOURS Dawn to Dusk

SIZE Small

GROUND Black Asphalt

DOG OWNER GROUP Dog Owners of Tribeca

CONTACT M. J. Bettenhausen

TEL (212) 732 9657

FISHBRIDGE PARK DOG RUN

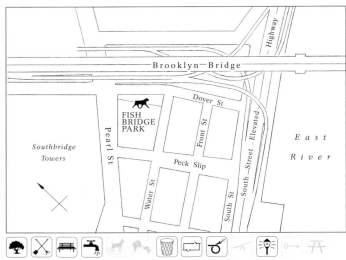

Dogs race the length of this narrow run to the far end where they catch a glimpse of the Brooklyn Bridge in the distance.

PARK FishBridge Park

LOCATION Pearl and Dover Streets

HOURS Dawn to Dusk

SIZE Small

GROUND Cement

DOG OWNER GROUP South-Water-Front Neighborhood Association

DONATIONS P.O. Box 279, Peck Slip Station, New York, NY 10272

CONTACT Gary Fagin

TEL (212) 267 5316

E-MAIL garyfagin@earthlink.net

BPC NORTH DOG RUN

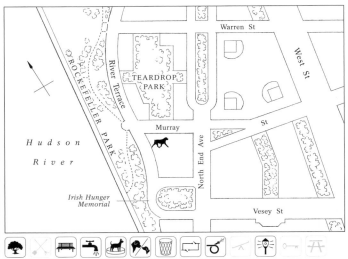

This temporary run awaits a permanent home nearby. Meanwhile, it is kept clean and pleasant for doggie visits.

LOCATION Murray Street and River Terrace

HOURS Dawn to Dusk

SIZE Small

GROUND Asphalt

DOG OWNER GROUP Battery Park City Dog Association

CONTACT Paula Galloway

E-MAIL bpcdogs@rundog.com

WEBSITE www.bpcdogs.org

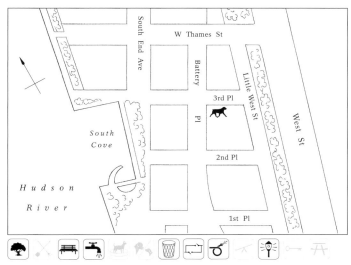

LOCATION Battery Place and Third Place

HOURS Dawn to Dusk

SIZE Small

GROUND Black Asphalt

DOG OWNER GROUP Battery Park City Dog Association

CONTACT Paula Galloway

E-MAIL bpcdogs@rundog.com

WEBSITE www.bpcdogs.org

This no-nonsense run is set up within a parking lot to be as convenient and user-friendly as possible until it is moved to a permanent site nearby.

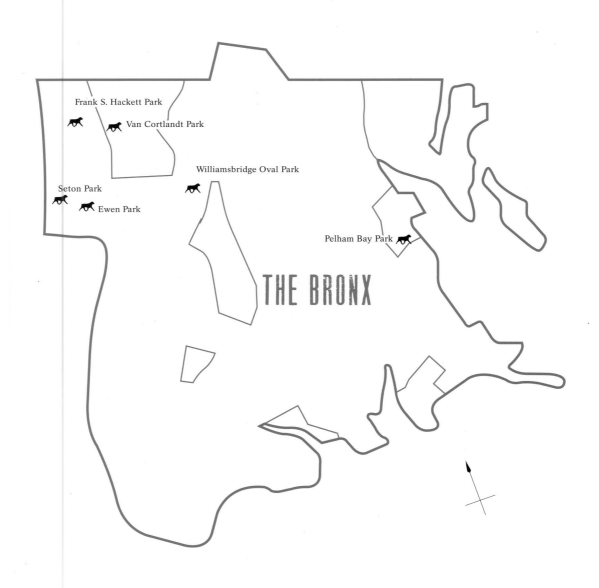

Frank S. Hackett Park

Van Cortlandt Park

Williamsbridge Oval Park

Seton Park

Ewen Park

Pelham Bay Park

THE BRONX

Early on Indy took great delight in unleashed play and relished trips to the dog run. But she also found great happiness in the exploration of city park trails, where she often came across one of dog-kind's greatest joys—the stick. A good stick can bring out deep-rooted dog desires. For some dogs, a stick means "chase, retrieve, and repeat," for others the ritual starts with chase and abruptly shifts to "chase me and try to get it back." Regular sticks could not hold Indy's interest for long. Only oversized sticks were worthy of her stature and could arouse something in her that was pure lumberjack.

The best chance to discover Indy's idea of a great stick was after a storm when branches had been freshly shaken from the trees. Indy's urge for order inspired her to develop a strategy for reaching her goal. Disassembling a branch begins with the smaller exterior shoots. Break them all off at the point where they emerge and toss aside. Growl at any non-compliance. Work a way in as far as possible, periodically shaking off bark and soft wood, to reveal a great stick. If it is large, balance and carry. If it is very large, lift and drag. If it is massive, tug a few inches, or just give the appropriate bark. That will suffice in showing who is master of the urban forest.

The Bronx is a fantastic place to find such canine attractions. It is home to an astonishing variety of trees including white, red, and black oaks, beeches, hickories, red maples, sweet gums, cherry, birch, linden, and tulip trees. Expansive nature trails offer plenty of opportunities for leashed walks. Pelham Bay Park is New York City's largest park by far with over 2,700 acres. Three times the size of Central Park, it encompasses a river, lagoon, marshes, and historical sites along its hiking trails. Van Cortlandt Park, the city's third largest park, offers miles of exquisite trails on 1,146 acres.

In addition to the opportunity to learn about native plant life, those on park hikes may also be treated to wildlife sightings. Many birds and animals, including woodpeckers, ducks, owls, bats, wild turkeys, white-tailed deer, rabbits, raccoons, opossums, skunks, chipmunks, and woodchucks inhabit the borough. Even coyotes are occasionally sighted in the Bronx, 24 percent of which is covered by parkland.

Bronx dog organizations like "Earth Angels, Canine Rescue" (www.earthangelsnyc.org) are active in using a network of volunteers to provide foster care for the borough's homeless dogs until permanent, loving homes are found. Their dogs are listed along with many other dogs for adoption on Petfinder (www.petfinder.org), an excellent resource serving New York City and beyond.

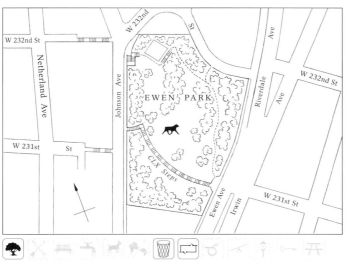

PARK Ewen Park

LOCATION West 231st Street and Johnson Avenue

HOURS Dawn to Dusk

SIZE Small

GROUND Wood Chips, Grass

To get involved in caring for this dog run contact:

The Partnerships for Parks Outreach Coordinator for this Park

ADDRESS c/o Partnerships for Parks,

830 Fifth Avenue—The Arsenal,

New York, NY 10021

TEL (718) 430 1861

WEBSITE www.partnershipsforparks.org

Dogs can lounge on a luxurious blanket of strong grasses under a truly spectacular tree in this otherwise basic run.

SETON DOG RUN

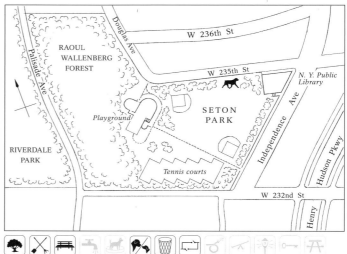

This long utilitarian run is neighbored to the rear by a newer additional run, which is more expansive and encircles trees and rocks in its landscape, and offers a feeling of sanctuary.

PARK Seton Park

LOCATION West 235th Street and Independence Avenue

HOURS Dawn to Dusk

SIZE Large

GROUND Wood Chips, Dirt

To get involved in caring for this dog run contact:

The Partnerships for Parks Outreach Coordinator for this Park

ADDRESS c/o Partnerships for Parks,

830 Fifth Avenue—The Arsenal,

New York, NY 10021

TEL (718) 430 1861

WEBSITE www.partnershipsforparks.org

FRANK'S DOG RUN

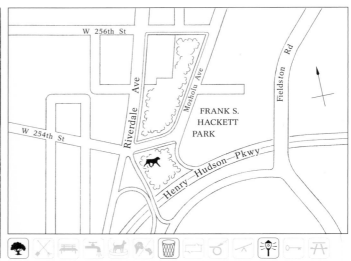

A great spot for a run, but the flimsy fence does not take in all the usable space. With no real room to run, the optimistic canine will engage in another favorite pastime, digging!

PARK Frank S. Hackett Park

LOCATION West 254th Street and Riverdale Avenue

HOURS Dawn to Dusk

SIZE Small

GROUND Dirt, Grass

To get involved in caring for this dog run contact:

The Partnerships for Parks Outreach Coordinator for this Park

ADDRESS c/o Partnerships for Parks,

830 Fifth Avenue—The Arsenal,

New York, NY 10021

TEL (718) 430 1861

WEBSITE www.partnershipsforparks.org

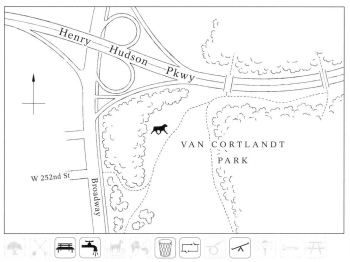

PARK Van Cortlandt Park

LOCATION West 252nd Street and Broadway

HOURS Dawn to Dusk

SIZE Large

GROUND Grass

DOG OWNER GROUP Friends of Canine Court

ADDRESS c/o City of New York Parks and Recreation,
1 Bronx River Parkway, Bronx, NY 10462

CONTACT Bash Dibra

TEL (718) 884 8238 or via Parks Department (718) 430 1890

E-MAIL bash@pawsacrossamerica.com

WEBSITE www.pawsacrossamerica.com

This run has a course with canine agility equipment, and is flanked by a run of equal size for dogs that want to just cheer from the benches or stretch out and play.

WILLIAMSBRIDGE OVAL DOG RUN 🐾🐾

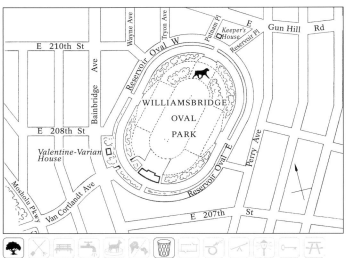

This run is located in a nice area, and could be made more appealing with a stronger fence and additional amenities.

PARK Williamsbridge Oval Park

LOCATION Reservoir Oval West and Putnam Place

HOURS Dawn to Dusk

SIZE Medium

GROUND Wood Chips

To get involved in caring for this dog run contact:

The Partnerships for Parks Outreach Coordinator for this Park

ADDRESS c/o Partnerships for Parks,

830 Fifth Avenue—The Arsenal,

New York, NY 10021

TEL (718) 430 1861

WEBSITE www.partnershipsforparks.org

PELHAM BAY DOG RUN

This dog run provides space for socializing and playing before and after excursions through the park's diverse landscape.

PARK Pelham Bay Park

LOCATION Middletown Road and Stadium Avenue

HOURS Dawn to Dusk

SIZE Small

GROUND Pea Gravel

To get involved in caring for this dog run contact:

Director of Community Outreach Marianne Anderson

ADDRESS c/o City of New York Parks and Recreation,
1 Bronx River Parkway, Bronx, NY 10462

TEL (718) 430 1890

E-MAIL Marianne.Anderson@parks.nyc.gov

Monsignor McGolrick Park

McCarren Park

Hillside Park

Palmetto Playground

Fort Greene Park

Dimattina Park

Prospect Park

BROOKLYN

Owl's Head Park

Dyker Beach Park

Seth Low Park

Manhattan Beach Park

When Indy blossomed into a true 120-pound lady, we moved to Williamsburg, Brooklyn. In place of the urban canyons that she left behind, Indy had a yard she could call her own and counted a doghouse and kiddie pool among her personal amenities. Nevertheless, almost everyday she would run alongside my bike—and regularly bring us both to a sudden and dangerous halt at the gutter—down Bedford Avenue to McCarren Park. There, after she was let loose, the bicycle would transform into a monster that Indy defended us from by chasing the back tire and attempting to bite it, all the while barking admonishments. At that time, the dog run in McCarren Park did not exist and we carried on with our eccentricities unquestioned. Indy's return visits to the neighborhood and park roused many a bark of greetings, for old time's sake.

As we discovered, dog life in Brooklyn straddles the best of both rural and urban worlds. There are parks to roam and enough doggie events to rival any Manhattan pup's social calendar. Even those lucky enough to live in homes with yards of their own are enticed to take advantage of area parks, dog runs, and events to keep up their social skills.

Committed dog owner groups in Brooklyn have been able to successfully support unleashed play in parks without dog runs. The Fellowship for the Interests of Dogs and their Owners (FIDO, www.fidobrooklyn.com) hosts several dog events in the gorgeous, 526-acre Prospect Park. The park is exceptionally dog friendly with extended unleashed hours, doggie drinking fountains, and a dog beach. Some events include Coffee Bark, a monthly social gathering; Pupnick, an annual doggie potluck picnic; and Bark the Herald Angels Sing, a chance for canine caroling. Additionally, the Fort Greene Park Users and Pets Society (PUPS, www.fortgreenepups.org) hosts events like an annual dog wash and the Great PUPkin Halloween Costume Contest. The group also works to keep the historic, 30-acre Fort Greene Park clean and dog friendly.

There are active, no-kill organizations such as Mighty Mutts (www.mightymutts.net) that help care for the borough and city's strays. The Brooklyn Animal Resource Coalition (BARC, www.barcshelter.org) even has a sponsorship program that allows one to meet the furry recipient of their support. BARC also hosts a popular annual dog parade and show to help support the shelter and celebrate the dogs of Brooklyn.

MCGOLRICK'S DOG RUN

The creation of this run was spurred on by the tragic death of a dog killed by a car in the park. Now lucky neighborhood dogs have a safe place all their own.

PARK Monsignor McGolrick Park

LOCATION Driggs Avenue and Russell Street

HOURS Dawn to Dusk

SIZE Medium

GROUND Wood Chips

DOG OWNER GROUP D.O.G. Association (Dogs of Greenpoint)

CONTACT Rachel Vicary

E-MAIL dogsofgreenpoint@yahoo.com

TEL via Partnerships for Parks, (718) 965 8907

MCCARREN DOG RUN

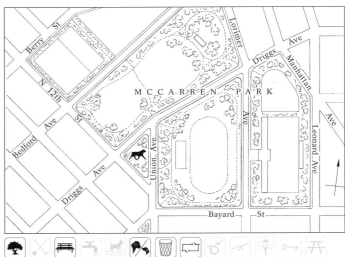

Though not formally organized, run users regularly pitch in to help maintain this run. Volunteer schedules are passed by word of mouth through the run's community.

PARK McCarren Park

LOCATION Driggs Avenue and North 12th Street

HOURS Dawn to Dusk

SIZE Medium

GROUND Wood Chips

To get involved in caring for this dog run contact:

The Partnerships for Parks Outreach Coordinator for this Park

ADDRESS c/o Partnerships for Parks,

830 Fifth Avenue—The Arsenal,

New York, NY 10021

TEL via Partnerships for Parks, (718) 965 8907

WEBSITE www.partnershipsforparks.org

HILLSIDE DOG PARK

🐾🐾🐾🐾

This is more than just a dog run; it is a dog park. Canines have the roam of the entire park for off-leash play.

PARK Hillside Dog Park

LOCATION Columbia Heights, Vine Street, and the BQE

HOURS 6 A.M. to 1 A.M.

SIZE Large

GROUND Wood chips, Grass, Dirt

DOG OWNER GROUP Friends of Hillside Dog Park

DONATIONS 111 Hicks Street, #5P, Brooklyn, NY 11201

CONTACT Muffet Jones

TEL via Partnerships for Parks, (718) 965 8907

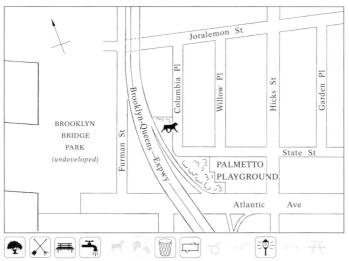

PARK Palmetto Playground

LOCATION Columbia Place and State Street

HOURS Dawn to Dusk

SIZE Small

GROUND Dirt

To get involved in caring for this dog run contact:

The Partnerships for Parks Outreach Coordinator for this Park

ADDRESS c/o Partnerships for Parks,

830 Fifth Avenue—The Arsenal,

New York, NY 10021

TEL via Partnerships for Parks, (718) 965 8907

WEBSITE www.partnershipsforparks.org

This charming run is a nice meeting spot for neighborhood dogs to socialize.

PARK Vincent J. Dimattina Park

LOCATION Hicks Street and Hamilton Avenue

HOURS Dawn to Dusk

SIZE Small

GROUND Crushed Granite

DOG OWNER GROUP Carroll Gardens D.O.G.S.

DONATIONS c/o Community Board 6, 250 Baltic Street, Brooklyn, New York 11201

CONTACT James Aridas

TEL (718) 625 1484

E-MAIL penquin325@msn.com

Beautiful landscaping and features adorn this run, which makes regular visits particularly pleasurable.

OWL'S HEAD DOG RUN

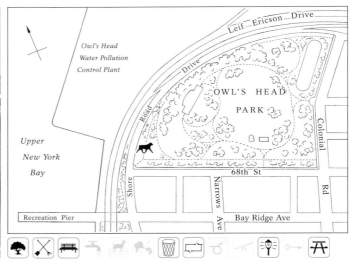

Visiting canines have room to race each other, the cars that go by, or even the passing ships, all within the safety of the dog run. This run has brought together people that do not always speak the same language, yet share a common love for dogs.

PARK Owl's Head Park

LOCATION Shore Road Drive and 68th Street

HOURS Dawn to Dusk

SIZE Medium

GROUND Dirt, Grass

DOG OWNER GROUP Friends and Neighbors of Owl's Head Park

DONATIONS 6821 Bliss Terrace, Brooklyn, NY 11220

CONTACT Bernadette Hoban

TEL (718) 745 4218

E-MAIL bhoban1@msn.com

PARK Dyker Beach Park

LOCATION 86th Street and 7th Avenue

HOURS Dawn to Dusk

SIZE Large

GROUND Grass

To get involved in caring for this dog run contact:

The Partnerships for Parks Outreach Coordinator for this Park

ADDRESS c/o Partnerships for Parks,

830 Fifth Avenue—The Arsenal,

New York, NY 10021

TEL (718) 965 8902

WEBSITE www.partnershipsforparks.org

This run puts smiles on the faces of its happy visitors. There is enough room here to play canine Frisbee and find inspiration to dream up new outdoor games for dogs.

SETH'S DOG RUN

*This dog run has few amenities.
Nonetheless, local dogs love getting
together here to socialize.*

PARK Seth Low Park

LOCATION Bay Parkway at 74th Street

HOURS Dawn to Dusk

SIZE Small

GROUND Wood Chips

To get involved in caring for this dog run contact:

The Partnerships for Parks Outreach Coordinator for this Park

ADDRESS c/o Partnerships for Parks,

830 Fifth Avenue—The Arsenal,

New York, NY 10021

TEL (718) 965 8992

WEBSITE www.partnershipsforparks.org

PARK Manhattan Beach Park

LOCATION Oriental Boulevard and Kensington Street

HOURS Dawn to Dusk

SIZE Large

GROUND Grass, Dirt

To get involved in caring for this dog run contact:

The Partnerships for Parks Outreach Coordinator for this Park

ADDRESS c/o Partnerships for Parks,

830 Fifth Avenue—The Arsenal,

New York, NY 10021

TEL (718) 965 8992

WEBSITE www.partnershipsforparks.org

Exhilarating breezes from the ocean gust into this spacious run where dogs play intensely.

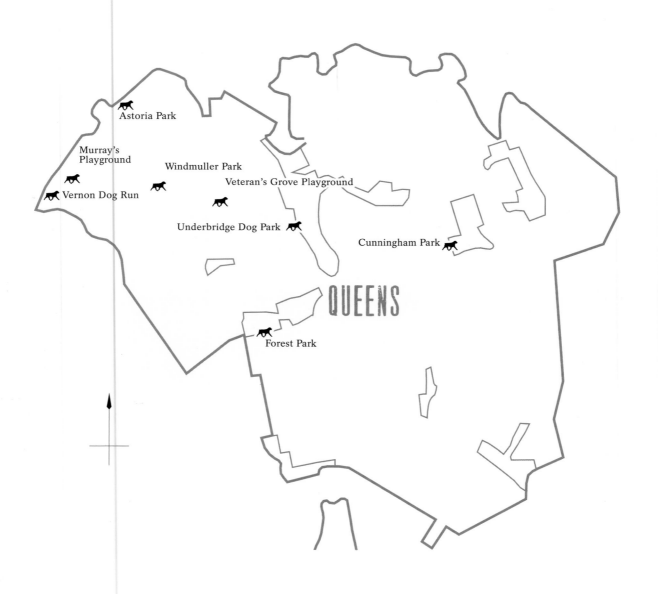

Astoria Park

Murray's
Playground

Windmuller Park

Veteran's Grove Playground

Vernon Dog Run

Underbridge Dog Park

Cunningham Park

QUEENS

Forest Park

We moved to Queens from Brooklyn and traded in our backyard for a larger apartment. Visits to Indy's new favorite place, Astoria Park, put to rest any uncertainties she may have had about the new address. She was getting older and preferred riding in the car to running beside the bike. Before each trip she would search for our car by sniffing every vehicle parked along the street. When she found it, her proud jumps announced her gleeful anticipation of a park excursion.

Being a cultured canine, Indy took great pleasure in the arts and she was particularly enthusiastic about visiting Socrates Sculpture Park in Queens. The outdoor space is a showcase for local sculptors whose rotating exhibits surprise and delight canines and humans alike. Indy's appreciation of art led her to circle each piece and investigate it from all possible perspectives. Her favorites included a giant metal ball as well as structures that she could climb into or pass through. The best journeys there always included the discovery of "found" pieces. They would range from abandoned old tires and orange construction cones to the most exciting—water sprinklers going full speed. Showing no fear, Indy would jump in the line of fire and bare her teeth at the source, as it became her giant water-pic.

Canine life in Queens can be fulfilling. There is art to ponder and nature to explore. With 7,106 acres of parkland distributed over 400 parks throughout the borough, there is a vast potential for on-leash "walkies." The 1,255-acre Flushing Meadows-Corona Park has hiking trails, meadows, marshlands, and two lakes. Alley Pond Park's 655 acres offer a diverse ecosystem for exploration with flora and fauna in saltwater and freshwater wetlands, kettle ponds, tidal flats, forests, and meadows. Forest Park's 538 acres include a 413-acre forest of native red and white oaks, with some trees that are more than 150 years old.

The Olympics are held in Queens, (the Dog Olympics, that is), a fall event hosted by Alley Pond Pet Lovers, APPL, a canine community that helps care for Alley Pond Park. Springtime brings the canine Easter bonnet contest held in Forest Park, and borough dog runs host fundraising parties and contests throughout the year.

Shelters in Queens work to educate the public about responsible pet ownership through special programs. For example, Animal Haven (www.animalhavenshelter.org) provides courses in positive reinforcement training. Bobbi and the Strays (www.bobbicares.petfinder.org), and the Noah's Ark Project (www.arkproject.com) reach out to communities by conducting workshops at area schools. Additionally, the American Foundation for Animal Rescue (AFAR, www.afarnyc.org) offers seminars and a working internship program through its Animal Behavior Center at the Queens Community Animal Shelter.

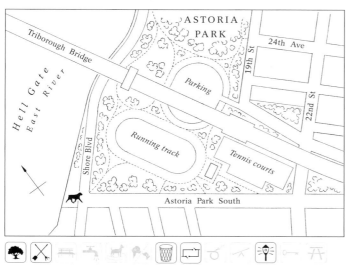

PARK Adjacent to Astoria Park

LOCATION Astoria Park South and Shore Boulevard

HOURS Dawn to Dusk

SIZE Small

GROUND Dirt, Grass

To get involved in caring for this dog run contact:

The Partnerships for Parks Outreach Coordinator for this Park

ADDRESS c/o Partnerships for Parks,

830 Fifth Avenue—The Arsenal,

New York, NY 10021

TEL (718) 520 5913

WEBSITE www.partnershipsforparks.org

Spots of fenced off greenery here are used as obstacles for outmaneuvering one's pursuers when "it" in games. This run is used and enjoyed by many dogs in the community. It is a nice, well-kept spot.

MURRAY'S DOG RUN 🐾 🐾

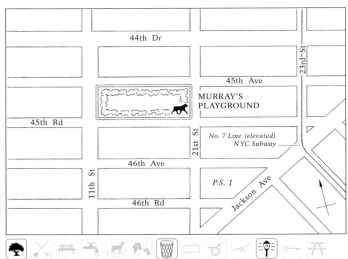

There is a large, weather worn sculpture inside this run. Dogs play around and under it, and contemplate the presence of this "Bigger Bird." This run is host to a high number of area dogs.

PARK John F. Murray Playground

LOCATION 21st Street and 45th Road

HOURS Dawn to Dusk

SIZE Medium

GROUND Dirt, Grass

To get involved in caring for this dog run contact:

Jeanne Molli at the Long Island City Inter-block Association

ADDRESS 21-03 45th Avenue,

LIC, NY 11101

TEL (718) 706 6584

VERNON DOG RUN

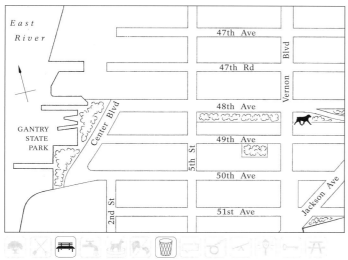

PARK Adjacent to Gantry Plaza State Park

LOCATION Vernon Boulevard and 48th Avenue

HOURS Dawn to Dusk

SIZE Medium

GROUND Wood Chips

DOG OWNER GROUP Friends of Gantry Plaza State Park

DONATIONS c/o City Lights at Queens Landing,
4–74 48th Avenue, LIC, NY 11109

CONTACT Rita Bradley

E-MAIL rjb0798@aol.com

BULLETINS www.queenswest.com

Although of decent size and clean, this run's amenities are kept at a minimum because it is temporary. Plans are underway to locate a permanent spot for the run within the Gantry Plaza State Park borders.

WINDMULLER DOG RUN

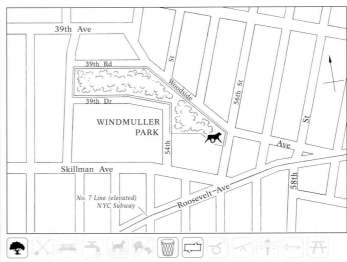

This run is not easily accessible, being in an out-of-the way area, on a small hill without steps. Nevertheless, some vivacious local dogs use it to tap into the pure joy of canine play.

PARK Windmuller Park

LOCATION 56th Street and Woodside Avenue

HOURS Dawn to Dusk

SIZE Small

GROUND Wood Chips, Dirt

To get involved in caring for this dog run contact:

The Partnerships for Parks Outreach Coordinator for this Park

ADDRESS c/o Partnerships for Parks,

830 Fifth Avenue—The Arsenal,

New York, NY 10021

TEL (718) 520 5913

WEBSITE www.partnershipsforparks.org

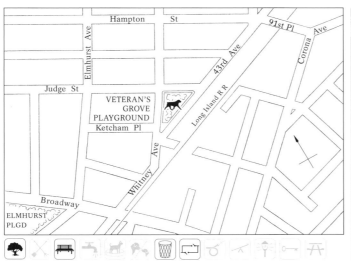

PARK Veteran's Grove Playground

LOCATION 43rd Avenue and Whitney Avenue

HOURS Dawn to Dusk

SIZE Small

GROUND Wood Chips, Dirt

To get involved in caring for this dog run contact:

The Partnerships for Parks Outreach Coordinator for this Park

ADDRESS c/o Partnerships for Parks,

830 Fifth Avenue—The Arsenal,

New York, NY 10021

TEL (718) 520 5948

WEBSITE www.partnershipsforparks.org

This long, narrow run offers no frills. However, just the chance to get out and sniff the other neighborhood dogs can be an important canine communication activity.

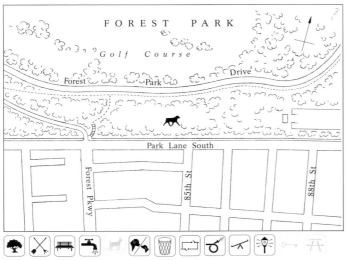

PARK Forest Park

LOCATION 85th Street and Park Lane South

HOURS 8 A.M. to 8 P.M.

SIZE Large

GROUND Bluestone Gravel

DOG OWNER GROUP K-9 Korral, Inc.

CONTACT Ronald Niles

TEL (718) 441 1940, or (917) 453 3283

E-MAIL k9korralfp@yahoo.com

WEBSITE http://geocities.com/k9korralfp

Over 500 active members use this run, which was once used as a corral for city patrol horses. Giant strides have been made here in creating a space that is a pleasure to visit for both canines and humans.

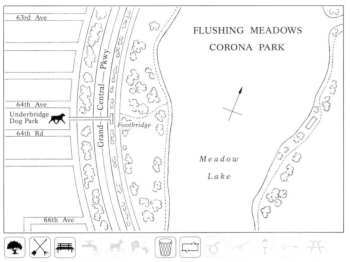

PARK Underbridge Dog Park

LOCATION 64th Avenue, West of the Grand Central Parkway

HOURS Dawn to Dusk

SIZE Large

GROUND Wood Chips

To get involved in caring for this dog run contact:

Park Manager William Gilbert

ADDRESS c/o The Overlook,

80–30 Park Lane,

Kew Gardens 11412

TEL (718) 699 4245

E-MAIL william.gilbert@parks.nyc.gov

The large horseshoe configuration of this park allows different groups of dogs to form when playing. Pine branches are occasionally chopped into the ground covering of wood chips, making it delightfully fragrant.

CUNNINGHAM DOG RUN

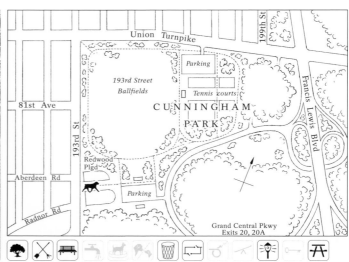

There is a charming stone pavilion bordering part of one side of the run. Several scattered trees provide shade, and serve as obstacles for breaking up the usual back and forth or one-way running play patterns.

PARK Cunningham Park

LOCATION 193rd Street and Aberdeen Road

HOURS Dawn to Dusk

SIZE Medium

GROUND Wood Chips

To get involved in caring for this dog run contact:

The Partnerships for Parks Outreach Coordinator for this Park

ADDRESS c/o Partnerships for Parks,

830 Fifth Avenue—The Arsenal,

New York, NY 10021

TEL (718) 520 5948

WEBSITE www.partnershipsforparks.org

STATEN ISLAND

Saint Peter's Church

The Greenbelt

Great Kills Park

Wolfe's Pond Park

With Indy serving as copilot of our trusty Volkswagen Jetta, her head hanging out of the window, her ears and tongue flapping in the wind, we sought canine activity on Staten Island. We discovered some private dog runs belonging to building complexes. In order to let your dog play there, however, one has to live on the premises, so we moved on in pursuit of more public possibilities. Soon, we located Wolfe's Run in Wolfe's Pond Park, which was established in 2003, and is the first public dog run on the island.

At Wolfe's Run, Indy and I witnessed familiar patterns of behavior exhibited by the visiting dogs. They displayed the same eagerness upon approaching the dog run that dogs show all over the city. Once within a whiff's distance of a run, dogs begin to shed the constraints of city life. Some canines race to meet their friends, pulling their person along on the leash, while others quiver in anticipation within the confines of special purses carried by their people. When free inside the run, dogs shift their behavior to that of emancipated canines. At the end of playtime, the whistle for the leash is met with dramatically different reactions. There may be pleading expressions for a time extension or a dashing match of "catch me if you can." Some dogs might even perform the classic "I did not hear that call" ignoring routine. For those who willingly come to the leash, the act of leaving friends is softened by the knowledge that a return tomorrow is part of their routine.

To accommodate the need for unleashed play, the Dog Owners Group of Staten Island (DOGSI, www.dogsi.org), has been advocating for more off-leash dog enclosures in the borough. Efforts are under way to open dog runs in Silver Lake and Clove Lake parks. Founders plan to dedicate the runs to Search and Rescue Dogs and other service dogs. Until then, we found that there is a whole world to discover while on leashed walks. The Staten Island Greenbelt maintains trails that pass through areas with open fields, meadows, woodlands, wetlands, swamps, glacial ponds, and lakes on its 2,800 acres of land. Great Kills Park welcomes dogs on leashes to visit the beach and take a dip in the water.

The Staten Island Council for Animal Welfare (SICAW, www.sicaw.petfinder.org) engages dogs and people in fun events and fundraising efforts such as yard sales, holiday pet photos with Santa and the Easter bunny, and an annual walk-a-thon to help care for the borough's homeless dogs.

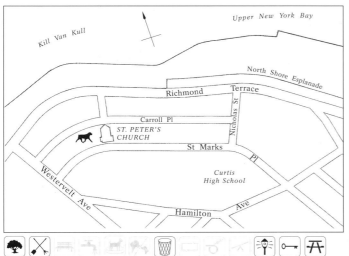

PLACE St. Peter's Church

LOCATION 53 St. Mark's Place

HOURS Dawn to Dusk

SIZE Large

GROUND Grass

DOG OWNER GROUP St. George's Canine Association

DONATIONS c/o St. Peter's Church, 53 St. Mark's Place, SI, NY 10301

CONTACT Bertram Ploog

TEL via St. Peter's Church, (718) 727 2672

MEMBERSHIP $100 Annual Dues

This is a beautiful environment with plenty of room and soft grass. Dogs that visit this immaculate run can relax to the sound of church bells. It is lovingly cared for by its users, and much appreciated by some of God's dearest creatures.

WOLFE'S DOG RUN

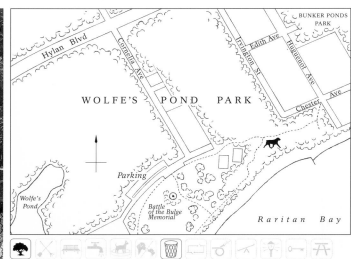

Pleasant paths meander toward this run, which is settled in a woodsy patch. Dog socialization and play here is soothed by the sounds of the ocean in the background.

PARK Wolfe's Pond Park

LOCATION Cornelia and Chester Avenues

HOURS Dawn to Dusk

SIZE Medium

GROUND Gravel

To get involved in caring for this dog run contact:

The Partnerships for Parks Outreach Coordinator for this Park

ADDRESS c/o Partnerships for Parks,

830 Fifth Avenue—The Arsenal,

New York, NY 10021

TEL (718) 390 8016

WEBSITE www.partnershipsforparks.org

START A DOG RUN

This is a summary of an article written by Jeffery Zhan, co-founder and president of the New York Council of Dog Owner Groups, NYCDOG, pronounced "nice dog," a powerful alliance that lobbies for unleashed canine recreation in the city. It was originally written for *Urbanhound: The New York City Dog's Ultimate Survival Guide*, by Nina Munk and Nadia Zonis. The complete article can be viewed at www.nycdog.org.

* **START A DOG OWNERS' GROUP** Begin by mobilizing local dog owners. Circulate a petition in your neighborhood to collect a few hundred names, addresses, telephone numbers, e-mail addresses, and occupations. Then register your group with the coordinator of volunteer efforts at the department of Parks and Recreation (call (212) 360 1310 or visit www.ci.nyc.ny.us/html/dpr/home.html).

* **PICK A SPOT** Almost any open space could work as a dog run. Identify more than one site and list pros and cons for each. Space on private land requires the owner's permission (located through your community board). Even privately owned sites may need public and government approval.

* **WRITE A PROPOSAL AND DRAW UP A PLAN** Outline the benefits of a dog run to the community at large, stating how and by whom it will be maintained, and include a sample set of dog run rules. Explain why your chosen site is ideal, but also include the pros and cons of other options. Include a rough budget and funding plan. Create a simple drawing showing how your run will fit in the surrounding area and include its basic components: fence line, water location, small dog area (many runs now incorporate this concept, or a second site can be used), benches, trees (with "tree benches" encircling them to protect the trees), gates (two entries are highly recommended and they should be "double gated" with a vestibule so that dogs don't run out when a single gate is open), and surface selection.

* **FIND THE FUNDS** A decent dog run—with basic drainage, surfacing, a sturdy fence and gates, benches, and source of water—will cost at least $50,000–$75,000. Maintenance (garbage bags, poop bags, periodic surface restoration, sanitation treatments, etc.) runs approximately $3,000–$5,000 a year in a public park, and far more in a private space (where you may need to pay for insurance and garbage collection). Once the project has been approved either the Parks Department will work with you to develop a budget and construction plan, or you can get help from NYCDOG.

  City Council members may have discretionary funds they can allocate to a dog run. The Parks Department often puts up partial funding for construction (but not for maintenance—dog owners cover that expense). And you can raise money from area dog owners, local merchants (especially pet-related), and companies that make pet products.

* **WORK THE SPHERES OF INFLUENCE** Write a letter stating your plan to the administrator of your park and send a copy to your Borough Commissioner, and the Commissioner of the Parks Department. Include a request for a meeting. Follow up by phone. In the case of a privately-owned site, contact the owner directly. Attend monthly Community Board meetings, appeal to your City Council members, State Assembly members, and State Senators (find them at www.nypirg.org).

* **GET APPROVED** In addition to the approval of the site's owner, get the approval of your Community Board. As the Community Board is a lightning rod for your opponents, be ready for complaints about unsanitary conditions, noise, odors, and more. Start a public relations campaign. Have your supporters, local veterinarians, NYCDOG, and celebrities attend (and speak at) Community Board meetings. Educate the community through newspapers, flyers, newsletters, and a website. Well before public approval meetings, target the Parks Department, elected officials, and ranking Community Board members with a letter-writing and phone-calling campaign.

* **KEEP UP THE GOOD WORK** Once the dog run is built, keep your group active for fundraising and clean-ups. Have regular meetings with the Parks Department and community officials to keep everyone involved and upbeat.

DESIGNING DOG RUNS

According to the American Kennel Club, the ideal dog run should include the following:

* One acre or more of land surrounded by a four- to six-foot high chain-link fence. The fence should be equipped with a double-gated entry to keep dogs from escaping and to facilitate wheelchair access.

* Cleaning supplies, including covered garbage cans, waste bags, and pooper-scooper stations.

* Shade and water for both dogs and owners, along with benches and tables.

* A safe, accessible location with adequate drainage and a grassy area that is mowed routinely.

* Signs that specify park hours and rules, and bulletin boards.

* Good lighting inside the run and area.

* Parking close to the site.

Grassy terrains are not always practical to maintain in New York City's dog runs. Because high traffic volume and nitrogen from dog urine kills grass, leaving dusty dirt and mud, another ground covering is usually required. Dog runs should have a soft surface that is durable, sanitary, and allows for good drainage and easy waste pick-up. Selection of surfacing depends on the run's size, budget, and the group of dog owners' preferences.

About various surface options:
* Crushed granite is durable, well draining, and soft on paws.
* Pea gravel hurts some dogs' paws, and provides spaces for bugs and fleas to hide.
* Quarter-inch pearl gravel mixed with rice gravel does not travel or hurt paws, and it drains well.
* Cement is easy to maintain and comes in decorative patterns, but is hard on joints and ligaments.
* Black asphalt gets too hot in the sun to walk on, and can tear the pads of paws.
* Clay chips and screenings can get dusty when dry and make stains when tracked home.
* Rubber padding and decking is expensive and may be difficult to clean.
* Wood chips absorb, and re-release odors, attracting bugs that like to bore into soft wood.

Dog run maintenance should include periodic treatments that are non-toxic to dogs, but kill parasites and odors. With many options to choose from, and new surfaces being regularly tested, visiting different runs and networking with other dog owner groups will assist the decision.

"Well organized dog runs, with members dedicated both to the well-being of their animal companions and their 'playgrounds,' have proven their potential to improve parks. On behalf of Parks & Recreation, I extend my gratitude to all dog owners who participate in dog run organizations. You make New York City's parks better places not only for your dogs, but also for all New Yorkers who love their green open spaces."

New York Parks & Recreation Commissioner Adrian Benepe

New York City is home to 28,700 acres of parkland. Parks are vital to the quality of urban life in that they offer an important break from the fast pace of the city. In just a few steps, one can move from cement under foot and steel towering overhead, to a seasonally changing feast for the eyes. Parks provide a chance to relax, breathe, and reconnect with nature, and one can share that experience with mankind's best friend.

With our leashed companions by our sides we can discover how diverse the land we live on really is, while learning about our environment and history. Parkland adventures take us through varied landscapes that offer picturesque views. Markers along the way identify a vast array of flora and fauna, and point out historical places and events.

Off-leash time in parks was established by former Commissioner Henry Stern for dogs under the control of their owners in late evenings and early mornings (before 9 A.M. and after 9 P.M.), when people are scarce. The presence of neighborhood "watch-dogs" contributes to safety in parks while providing dogs with access to nature. Be sure to check if the park you visit observes these "courtesy hours" or risk a ticket. By law, all dogs must be on a leash no longer than six feet at all times except in official, enclosed dog runs.

Dog runs are a relatively recent phenomenon in New York City. The first one opened in the early 1990s in Tompkins Square Park, and is fittingly named First Run. Most dog runs are given the nickname of the person in whose namesake park they reside. They are being increasingly designed into park plans from the outset because of the many benefits they provide. Dog runs create an effective way for dog owners to participate in preserving their community's parks while engaging in their chosen form of recreation.

Opposite is Balto, a hero dog who saved many human lives through his valiant bravery and courage.
His commemorative statue stands proudly in Central Park, at 67th Street and 5th Avenue, just inside the park.

Thank you to all the dogs and their people who allowed us to observe and photograph their dog run rituals. A very special thank you is extended to all the dog owners who work to create, organize, and keep dog runs safe and pleasant.

I am fortunate to have the mark of the winged horse of Prestel grace this book. Prestel's creative and visionary team is dedicated to the highest quality of work. Thank you Jürgen Tesch, Jürgen Krieger, Curt Holtz, Stephen Hulburt, Raya Raitcheva, and Evelyn Lee.

The maps of cartographer George Colbert are sure to be valued as treasure maps by New York City's dog owners. Petra Lüer's inspired design creates the perfect balance of artful and useful pages.

It is a privilege to include articles by professionals committed to the humane care of our pets. Dr. Stephen Zawistowski eloquently brings deeper understanding to the human-canine relationship. Dr. Sally Haddock graciously shares important information about the physical health of canines visiting dog runs.

The American Kennel Club, a prominent canine organization, shares its knowledge and experience concerning dog runs to the benefit of readers. Jeffery Zahn of NYCDOG continues to lead the pack on starting a dog run. Nina Munk's kind allowance to use Zahn's article on starting a dog run from her book *Urbanhound* is greatly appreciated.

The New York City Parks Department's dedication to responsible dog ownership is expressed in Parks and Recreation Commissioner Adrian Benepe's message to dog owners. Many thanks go to Dana Molina, Director of Volunteer Programs at Partnerships for Parks, for providing contacts for those interested in participating in dog runs in their communities' parks. Partnerships for Parks is a joint program of the City Parks Foundation and the New York City Department of Parks & Recreation. The Partnership engages community support and involvement in New York City Parks' activities.

Roy DeCarava has taught me much about the art of photography and his continued support and friendship are invaluable. The art of writing is a newer experience for me, and I am grateful for the skillful insights of my talented friends Andrea Quong, Neil Laird, and Josepha Conrad.

Many people generously shared experiences, encouragements, and support for this project. Some that really stand out include Martin, Christine, and Emma Codd, Johann Conforme, Beth Kimmerlie, Suzanne Latour, Reiner Leist, Emer Martin, Mary Panzer, Jim Riggio, Steve Riggio, Wilson Santiago, Tamara Staples, Erica Thompson, and Guenter Vollath.

I am most grateful to my family. Especially to Linda Sheridan, my mother, for unlimited support and encouragement, and to my husband, Tristan G. Sheridan, whose love sustains me and whose creative ideas have influenced all of these pages.

If you have a dog, I hope this book will inspire you to participate in your local dog run or start one. If you are considering taking on the responsibility of a companion animal, please adopt. In addition to your local shelter, the ASPCA (www.aspca.org), Petfinder (www.petfinder.org), and the Mayor's Alliance for NYC's Animals (www.animalalliancenyc.org) can help you find your perfect pal.

IN MEMORY OF INDY

This book was completed in the memory of our dog Indy,

who left this life as a result of cancer.

She was the inspiration, reason, and partner for this project.

Indy was our greatest companion in all adventures.

A fierce beauty, she was loving, intelligent, and sensitive.

We miss her dearly and are thankful that her canine path crossed ours.

The runs that were photographed for this book may or may not be in official legal standing. Always check the status of the area you intend to let your dog off leash in order to avoid a ticket. The conditions described are as perceived at a particular time, and may or may not be current. The canine photographs are not necessarily placed next to the runs where they were taken.

© Prestel Verlag, Munich · Berlin · London · New York, 2005

Map illustrations by George Colbert, New York
Photographs on pages 9 and 159 courtesy of
Tristan G. Sheridan, New York

Prestel Verlag
Königinstrasse 9, 80539 Munich
Tel. +49 (89) 38 17 09-0
Fax +49 (89) 38 17 09-35
www.prestel.de

Prestel Publishing Ltd.
4, Bloomsbury Place, London WC1A 2QA
Tel. +44 (020) 7323-5004
Fax +44 (020) 7636-8004

Prestel Publishing
900 Broadway, Suite 603
New York, N.Y. 10003
Tel. +1 (212) 995-2720
Fax +1 (212) 995-2733
www.prestel.com

Library of Congress Control Number: 2005900729

The Deutsche Bibliothek holds a record of this publication in the Deutsche Nationalbibliografie; detailed bibliographical data can be found under: http://dnb.ddb.de

Prestel books are available worldwide. Please contact your nearest bookseller or one of the listed addresses for information concerning your local distributor.

Design and layout by WIGEL, Munich
Origination by Reproline Genceller, Munich
Printed and bound by Sellier, Freising

Printed in Germany on acid-free paper
ISBN 3-7913-3261-9